Herbert Puchta and Günter Gerngross

AT THE ZOO

Hello, I'm Lizzie, and I'm at the zoo today! My favourite animals are the monkeys. What are your favourite animals?

Illustrated by Cristiano Lissoni

BEFORE READING

1 **Draw and colour the animals.**

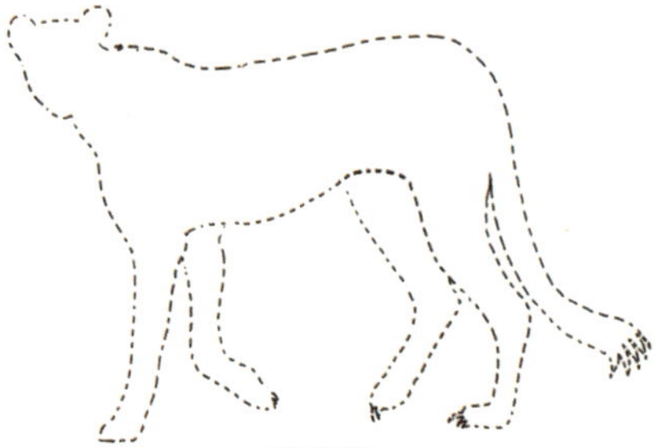

cheetah

monkey

elephant

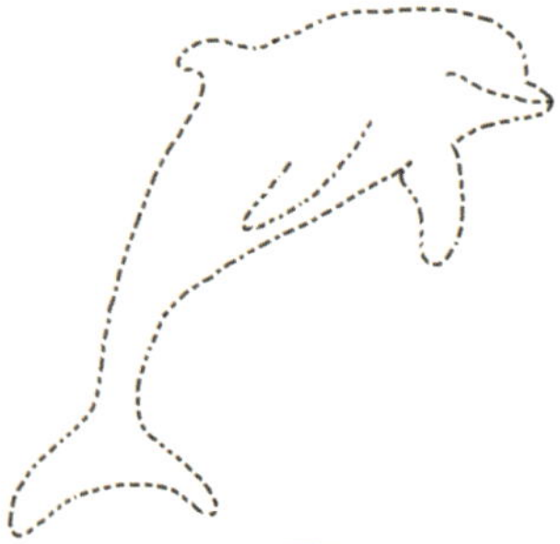

dolphin

hippo

2 **Say hello to the animals. Write in the balloons.**

A

B

C

D

E

Hello, monkey.
Hello, elephant.
Hello, cheetah.
Hello, dolphin.
Hello, hippo.

3 **Listen and point.**

First there are the monkeys.
The baby monkey is very friendly.
The monkey is right!
He can climb.
Lizzie's happy.

MIME
Can you climb like a monkey?

Now Lizzie and her mum are at the dolphin pool.

Splash!
The dolphin can swim and jump and he can splash!
Lizzie's wet, but she's happy.

HELLO, LIZZIE. LOOK! I CAN SWIM AND JUMP.

Lizzie and her mum
are at the elephants.
They are very big.
The elephant can lift a tree.
The elephant is very big
and very strong.

SPEAK

Are you strong? How many books can you lift?

Then Lizzie and her mum are at the hippos.
The hippo's very hungry!
He can eat lots of grass!

SPEAK

Are you hungry?
What would you like to eat?

In the evening Lizzie's in bed. She's thinking.

MUM, I'M NOT LIZZIE!

OH YES, YOU ARE!

SPEAK
Who is Lizzie?

AFTER READING

 1 Write the names next to the animals. Match them to their homes.

A 1

B 2

C 3

D 4

E 5

2   Listen and point.

3   What can they do? Write the names of the animals.

can run	can swim	can fly	can climb

AFTER READING

 4 **What can they do? Look and write.**

A I can fly.
I can climb.
....
....

B I can jump.
   I can run very fast.
   ....
   ....

5 **What about you? Write and tell a friend.**

I am Super.. .

I can ....   I can ....

I can ....   I can ....

AFTER READING

6 **Put in order from small to tall. Draw the pictures and write the names.**

small   tall

7 In the sky, on the land or in the water? Look and draw lines.

A

B

C

D

E

F

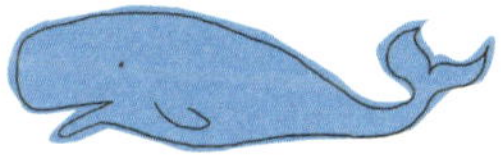

 8 Listen and point.

AFTER READING

 9 What are the names of the animals? Tell a friend.

 10 Listen and point to the animals.

A

B

C

D

E

F

 11 Where are their homes? Draw lines.

G

H

I

J

K

MAKE AND DO

Animal masks

Make animal masks.

You need:

colouring pencils

elastic

puncher

scissors

1 Download the animal masks from **The Thinking Train** website.

2 Carefully cut out the masks.

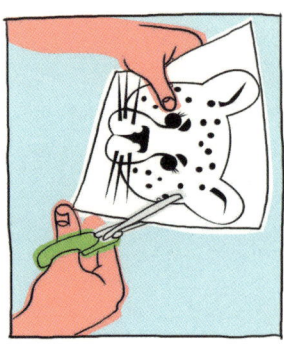

3 Colour the masks.

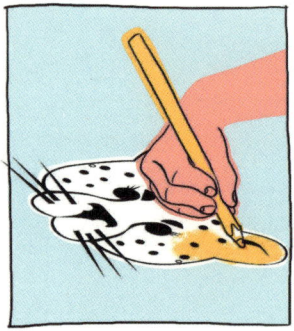

4 Punch out holes.

5 Tie some elastic to the masks.

6 Wear your masks and become zoo animals.